Octaves

for the Violin

Book One

by Cassia Harvey

CHP166

©2006 by C. Harvey Publications All Rights Reserved.

www.charveypublications.com - print books
www.learnstrings.com - PDF downloadable books
www.harveystringarrangements.com - chamber music

Octaves for the Violin 1

Book One

By Cassia Harvey
Edited by Myanna Harvey

Oh, Susannah
Foster

©2006 C. Harvey Publications All Rights Reserved

2

Alborada — Rimsky-Korsakov

3

Simple Gifts — Trad.

Octaves for the Violin, Book One

5

Canon — Tallis

6

Taps — Butterfield

7

She'll Be Coming Round the Mountain — Trad.

8

The Snouts and Ears of America — Trad.

9

Quadrille — Trad.

10

Go Tell Aunt Rhody — Trad.

Octaves for the Violin, Book One

11

The Blacksmith — Trad.

Octaves for the Violin, Book One

13

The Battle Cry of Freedom — Trad.

14

Across the Western Ocean — Trad.

15

Farandole — Bizet

Fine

D. C. al Fine

The Spider Song — Trad.

16

Aiken Drum — Trad.

17

Old Joe Clark — Trad.

18

Row, Row, Row Your Boat — Trad.

20

Camptown Races — Foster

21

Lightly Row — Trad.

22

Ode to Joy — Beethoven

Octaves for the Violin, Book One

23

My Bonny Lies Over the Ocean — Trad.

24

Drill Ye Tarriers, Drill   Trad.

Octaves for the Violin, Book One

25

Arkansas Traveler — Trad.

26

Danse Bacchanale — Saint-Saens

28

Ukranian Folk Song — Trad.

29

Blue-Eyed Girl — Trad.

30

Don Giovanni — Mozart

31

Country Gardens — Trad.

32

33

34

available from **www.charveypublications.com**: CHP246

Fourth Position for the Violin

by Cassia Harvey

A. First Shifting on the A String

B. First Shifting on the E String

©2014 C. Harvey Publications All Rights Reserved.

www.ingramcontent.com/pod-product-compliance
Lightning Source LLC
Chambersburg PA
CBHW051427070526
44584CB00023B/3623